Troy, Unincorporated

PHOENIX POETS

FRANCESCA ABBATE

Troy, Unincorporated

THE UNIVERSITY OF CHICAGO PRESS

Chicago & London

FRANCESCA ABBATE is associate professor of English at Beloit College. Her poetry has appeared in *Field*, *Iowa Review*, *NEO*, and *Poetry*, among others.

The University of Chicago Press, Chicago 60637
The University of Chicago Press, Ltd., London
© 2012 by The University of Chicago
All rights reserved. Published 2012.
Printed in the United States of America
21 20 19 18 17 16 15 14 13 12   1 2 3 4 5

ISBN-13: 978-0-226-00120-3 (paper)
ISBN-10: 0-226-00120-2 (paper)

Library of Congress Cataloging-in-Publication Data
Abbate, Francesca, author.
    Troy, unincorporated / Francesca Abbate.
        p. cm.
    Includes bibliographical references.
    ISBN-13: 978-0-226-00120-3 (paperback : alkaline paper)
    ISBN-10: 0-226-00120-2 (paperback : alkaline paper)
    1. Troy (Walworth County, Wis. : Town)—Poetry.   2. Chaucer,
Geoffrey, d. 1400. Troilus and Criseyde—Parodies, imitations, etc.
I. Title.
    PS3601.B357T76 2012
    811'.6—dc23   2011041481

⊛ This paper meets the requirements of ANSI/NISO Z39.48-1992
(Permanence of Paper).

For my parents

and

For Dan

Wherfore I biseke yow mekely, for the mercy of God, that ye preye for me that Crist have mercy on me and foryeve me my giltes; / and namely of my translacions and enditynges of worldly vanitees, the whiche I revoke in my retracciouns: / as is the book of Troilus.

Geoffrey Chaucer, "The Parson's Tale"

We are confused, the editors themselves complain, at the apparent anonymity of the messenger who opens the poem, and by the inconsistencies in reference in what should be a complete love letter.

Seth Lerer, "Envoy," *Chaucer and His Readers*

Troy, WI (Unincorporated)
Total 35.4 sq mi (91.8 km²)
Land 34.7 sq mi (90.0 km²)
Water 0.7 sq mi (1.8 km²)
Elevation [1] 915 ft (279 m)
Population (2000)
Total 2,328
Density 67.0/sq mi (25.9/km²)
Time zone Central (CST) (UTC-6)
Summer (DST) CDT (UTC-5)

CONTENTS

FOUR

ACKNOWLEDGMENTS

Grateful acknowledgment to the editors of the journals in which the following poems appeared, sometimes in different form:

Field: "[Psyche:] On the walls, the usual Americana" (as "Psyche's First Chili Dog"), "[Criseyde:] Dear (you know I never / rode horses well)," "[Troilus:] Nightfall when I crossed" (as "Progress")

The Iowa Review: "[Psyche's Song:] Praise me, I told the water lilies, for I am half-invincible" (as "Bog Song"), "[Chorus:] Then came the sand trucks" (as "Reconstruction"), "[Chorus:] The way fences open" (as "Dispatch")

The Journal: "[Criseyde:] How sadly my friends and I" (as "August, a Short Story"), "[Cassandra:] The halo—no mere incandescence" (as "Bridge, River, River, Bridge")

Poetry: "[Chorus:] Everything is half here" (as "Unusually Warm March Day, Leading to Storms"), "[Chorus:] We tried to remember" (as "The Envoy")

Thanks to the people—too numerous to list—who have provided advice, wisdom, and friendship over the years, including my teachers at the University of Montana, the University of Wisconsin–Milwaukee (and particularly Xavier Baron, whose course introduced me to *Troilus and Criseyde*), the Colrain Manuscript Conference, the Vermont College Postgraduate Writer's Conference, my colleagues and students at Beloit College, and Robert Firth. Thanks to Zoie Keithley and Anne Shaw for encouragement, and to Steve Daniels for the companionship of the shop—and for the telescope. To Linda Gregerson, enduring gratitude.

[CHORUS:]

This false world,—allas!—who may it leve?
—Chaucer, *Troilus and Criseyde* (II.420)

Everything is half here,
like the marble head
of the Greek warrior
and the lean torso
of his favorite.
The way the funnel cloud
which doesn't seem
to touch ground does—
flips a few cars, a semi—
we learn to walk miles
above our bodies.
The pig farms dissolve,
then the small hills.
As in dreams fraught
with irrevocable gestures,
the ruined set seemed larger,
a charred palace
the gaze tunnels through
and through. How well
we remember the stage—
the actors gliding about
like petite sails, the balustrade

cooling our palms.
Not wings or singing,
but a darkness fast as blood.
It ended at our fingertips.
The fence gave way.
The world began.

One

And so bifel, whan comen was the tyme
Of Aperil, whan clothed is the mede
With newe grene, of lusty Veer the pryme,
And swote smellen floures white and rede,
In sondry wises shewed, as I rede,
The folk of Troie hire observaunces olde,
Palladiones feste for to holde.

Chaucer, *Troilus and Criseyde* (1.155–61)

[PSYCHE'S SONG:]

Praise me, I told the water lilies, for I am half-invincible,
half-destructible, half-mad: am, in fact, a divine half

and a half not, and it's lonely out here and hot,
and half a lifetime has elapsed on this floating path

with its canopy of poison sumac, its pale, half-dead
orchids, the dreams of bog people hidden

under the planks—so finely pored, so stubble-bladed,
so adept at heat and loneliness, so not half—for who

will praise me now, I who was too clever by half,
who had an idea but no map: narrowing road, clearing,

the sun like the secret shining in the dark halves of all things,
like the improbable spirit—house in a wood,

wet seed under the weight of thought?

[NARRATOR:]

Of eighth grade—
        tried reading the *Comedies*,
as if to live in the forest naming the flowers
and flighty things when really

I was a fat girl
hurtling the length of a shotgun apartment
and crying bullet! when she leapt.

The photo recalls me thus: of vellum, a gulping sheen,

a blot under the crucifix
in her red velvet blazer.
        Homeroom: paper plates, lemonade,
someone's pink-candled birthday cake—

I stayed at my desk. Penned, making real
        progress:

        Once she watched a house burn and thought
        a commotion of flamingos.
        Once the spring trees cast such delirious nets
        she left someone
        for someone with his hand on the next big thing
        and that was sexy.

Dear So-and-So,
I wanted to be a real scholar.

Then March. Then April
signed its proclamation of cloud—

[CRISEYDE:]

How sadly my friends and I
go after the fallen straps
of our tank tops
as if worn by some

dawning nostalgia
for the way the wind
gets to the picnic table
where we've set

the Campari and soda
the bowl of potato chips
the bowl of green olives

Afternoon's in the offing

we're a small herd
grazing small-ly
not Edenic not like gazelles
though by the dead tree

whose base has been boxed
and seeded with nasturtiums
and morning glories
Helen raises a quick finger

to the weather's indifference
I hear you   what's to love is
a good question
For me it's laziness

sure   But also a stoicism
I was an orb gliding
over the town's pale rivers
the sun in her corner

queenly   a dead pearl

[PANDARUS:]

Troilus I said we're just dumb boys you know
the sound of a loose ball joint on a broken road
but as for will or won't she leave it to fate
I said and me I said I'll help

All afternoon I sat on his bed
watching the kite festival in the park
its snakes flashing through high clouds

Tending him Troilus feverish Troilus a litany
of whens a boy with clocks for brains

But I told myself someday you'll wake
less Troilus and the thought was like waking
to an accordion dawn
like I grew another pair of eyes
that opened on another room coastal full
of bone light and the smell of something cold
and mere something (funny) like raw squid

And I was a story shut inside this
remembering Troilus kite-tossed
in his sheets and how the garden
that day was more wind than green

Troilus listen I said between the words
"tree" and "bur oak" a forest sidles in
I don't know what I meant

I was thinking "girl": "Cressid" thinking
"April": Troilus finally dying like the rest of us

[TROILUS:]

Sniffly weather, the sky all prologue.
Lean hard from the hilltop
so the wind can catch you.

I stayed in bed, Pandarus quoting old potions
from Pliny to make me laugh:

"Wolf's liver in thin wine,
lard of a sow fed upon grass—
or was it the flesh of a she-ass
taken in broth?"

My ribs quaked so coughing I imagined
the boat of me after.
The river crumpled

like sheets someone couldn't crawl from
fast enough. I told him:

Pliny's also known for choking to death
on the ashes of Mt. Vesuvius.

I told him: Criseyde at the picnic in the rain
in her black dress.

I stayed in bed and I think

I slept, Pandarus narrating my dreams
like a radio play I got in fits:

meat and the mouth and the hand that fed you
petal shroud door in the garden
harbinger harbinger

the dial sliding back and forth
until, when I woke, the windows
were frost-cast

and he was on his feet,
muttering something about how
we had a house to build now.

He handed me the pewter vase
from the nightstand to spit up in.

Something dry down there.
Fly husk, I guessed, or maybe
an old stem bit?

No, a scrap of paper
balled tight.
Hocus Pocus. Here is the body—
I fished it out. I ate it.

[CRISEYDE:]

In those days arrows were *very* magic
                you woke a pomp of bone and tinsel
fluttering on someone's pretty strings

You woke a foreign empire
                antique, the wharf rats legion,
the messengers doff such funny hats

All the graffiti says *find me find*
                your irrevocably dazzled thing
In her heart, Psyche calls the city Citrine

She's grown all attention—
                under eyes saffron, lovely
clavicle, sweet each rib

Before bed she puts a piece of bread
                on the windowsill where daily
she studies the smokestacks

the lean of anonymous trees
                What crumb dawn finds
says she had a mooring, a morning,

a house in a wood with a lacquered bedroom
        and goldfinches dizzying the ceiling
The jewelry box on the nightstand

played "Lara's Theme"
        She liked taking the bottom off to watch
how the drum spun under the teeth

A commonplace, that the soul can't
        tell human time
See, you're not the fence, she'd say

I'm not your sheep

[PSYCHE:]

On the walls, the usual Americana.
The place was half under
the sidewalk, I'd nearly missed
the five cement stairs down.

In those lake cities
dusk affords year-round
a winterish distance.

It was winter anyway, very—
every cardinal like the throat
in the pulse of sleep.

She sleeps, she slept, she will sleep.
When I woke it was like a holiday.
Everything was shut.

     You should eat something,
the voice said. Not yours—
my body maybe.
But I'm a traveler, I said,
I travel, I do not want.

So I ordered a chili dog,
which I particularly did not want.

I sat at the counter, under the girl
in polka dots and white gloves
sharing a Coke with Mr. Sailor,
her never-lover.

A commonplace, to feel meant
for something. Another: to feel un-
meant, like: the boat's gone,
that thought you thought
you belonged to.

The wax cup of root beer
in my hand was as cold
as my hand: I could neither warm
nor relinquish it.

Go on, the voice said, *eat*.

Not yours. Some ant god, maybe,
shepherd of another petty hour.

I wiped mustard from the tips of my hair,
onions from my lap.
I licked someone else's stray poppy seeds
from my fingers.

In the waxpaper-lined plastic basket,
jetsam—a wreckage of napkins.
Between such crafts we bide.

[PANDARUS:]

We made a sand woman on Harrington Beach
in junior high a curving groove filled
with two mounds a hole

I poured half my Coke in
double double toil and trouble

I bet when Troilus comes
it's still some giant wave
thrusting him on shore not ours

(weed-roped piles of alewives
gulls have reaped the eyes from)

Bougainvillea starfish pink sand
I know I shouldn't think this

It's my job I said I fix things

We were in line for popcorn
Criseyde saving our seats
admiring her nails probably
I'd chosen the movie
Zombies but funny so post-credits
we wouldn't mistake
the strip mall's parking lot
for one of hell's minor antechambers

Troilus less in the movie
than in her hair and *well begun
is half done* I thought

When he surfaced
the look on his face
looked permanent

a portrait governed

I gave him the keys

Said I wanted to walk just drop it
tomorrow at the shop
that was the Z car
I sold last month it didn't idle
so much as strain to be let off leash

I figured she'd be impressed
if he could handle it

I had the valve job on the Volvo to get to
in the morning

And I wanted to think about the movie
guy ends up keeping his zombied friend
in the shed to play video games with

A small cold windless rain no bugs
crooning *yes it's only a canvas sky*
hanging over a muslin tree
to the streetlights

No raccoon-scuffle in the garbage cans

We're greedy if brief

Two

Ful redy was at prime Diomede
Criseyde unto the Grekis oost to lede,
For sorwe of which she felt hire herte blede,
As she that nyste what was best to rede.
And trewely, as men in bokes rede,
Men wiste nevere womman han the care,
Ne was so loth out of a town to fare.

Chaucer, *Troilus and Criseyde* (V.15–21)

[CASSANDRA:]

The halo—no mere incandescence—
is the brand of the terribly
fucked, the soon-

to-be-devoured. Nor do we suffer
accordingly, but beyond that,
in the realm of the "really interesting,"

the desert, say, the dusky kitchen
where knives sing. Even a vaguer
dissatisfaction marshals the sky,

as, in a museum in the Alps,
one might study a model of the Alps
casting its own shadows to scale.

"If the best thing about the mountains
is our thoughts of the mountains,
we're all fucked." Or so P. says,

cutting his nails by streetlight
as the cottonwoods flutter and fade
and T. pencils sad and busy heads

on the backs of all the envelopes.
The lull, that predicament of ghosts,
catches the map of the minute

at wow, two eternities.

The afternoon grew taller when a boy on Halsted
hoisted his slim friend for a twirl
and yelled—a sweet growl, really—
Jenny, you're a fucking porch pickle!
We were walking home from the zoo,
where who doesn't swoon
over the seal's big love-me look.
But have you noticed, I asked Dan,
that all seals look like seals looking out
of seal costumes? Ours were cows—
gray, or mottled pewter, rather.
You could go down the slippery stairs
to watch them underwater, and *Look!*,
a boy put his finger on the luminous
wall, *it pooped!* Of course time only
in retrospect stills. As in: funny, but I still
see most clearly—from a tail
like two thick furred palm fronds—that seal poop
feathering its way to the bottom of the pool.
After Jenny's tipsy spin, I took the day's
only photo—Dan in his new straw hat
under the bee-laden linden—
and taking it remembered: shadowing
this photo was another, fifteen years older
of my ex-husband in his new July panama.

Too bad the pigtailed girl at Dan's knee—
her lips one unmatchable shade
of popsicle blue—just missed the frame.
In even fleeting grief, the world's a copy of.
Fingernails, lace: such small stuff betrays the forger.

[CRISEYDE:]

Like the friend following you
into the thrall of the park by night—

through the gazebo and the swings
to the slide—
that *no, you go* caught in my hair.

A gray epoch. Rain smoke. Stars
in the black gutters when it cleared.
My dreams grew big with whales
and buck-teethed women
whose veiled hats kept them kindly
at a distance.

I opened all the doors in the house
to collect light. Pale doors. Pale floors.
I wanted to turn ghost or water.

He's mopey, the story said
one morning, *but you like him right?*
I was eating breakfast. Recounting,
on the neighbor's lawn,
the thinning herd of plastic deer.

*Tell me more about the salt trade,
I'm bored,* I said, *tell me anything.*

The cat settled into her pillow on the bed.
Juice stung my wrist—the story'd stolen
another bite of nectarine.

It liked making me blush. It liked:
the ribbon shoelaces on my high heels,
certain frequencies of cloud, the parrot
who said only *No more good time Charlie for you!*

Before he came. After he left.
The girls at the beauty school
gossiping over their mannequin heads.

[TROILUS:]

I was a boy. I listened to frog song
all one night and decided:
we wear clothes as courtesy, as kindness.

As if, behind the doors of today's shirt
were an unfurnished noon.
Spoon-colored sky under muslin.
Pigeon chat. Interior, in short,
with sudden snow.

Yesterday I walked out to see
what the receding river left,
wishing for the mud and tumble of deck chairs
and hubcaps and single-engine planes.

I found globes of plastic netting—
the kind used to buffer Asian pears.

When I was a boy, I asked for a map
of the moon and I learned:
the moon is horsed, but motherless.

Its horses are like pebbles
the current took the color from.
Ochre, wood-ash, less than dun.
So silly small and ghostly

their trail might be a flush
of ants across your feet.

But they run and they run
and they make everything the moon is:
dust and craters and mountains

and shine. I was a boy.
I believed what Beauty said.

[CRISEYDE:]

Already I miss Troy
in the summer.
My body propped
on the raft at Booth Lake,
feet stirring the weeds.

Population: a man
pulling a child's wagon
into the soyfield.
Seven hundred and twenty-six
red-winged blackbirds.
Two balloons tied to a stop sign
over a cardboard arrow
pointing down some dust snake
of a road.

In the summer
I wear my tube top
and Troilus takes me
to the drag races.

We sat late on the hot hood
of his car, his finger writing "wheel"
on my knee and
   believe me, believe me
said the floodlights.

On the way home,
a bloodied boy pissing
on his downed opponent's feet.

Pandarus in the back seat
telling stories.
   Hey, remember when Cassandra . . . etc., etc.
Old Pandarus.
Old word-scuttler.

Unseasonable, unreasonable,
my dad says of the heat.
I steady him in the walker
so he can hold a wrist under the tap,

the wet plate in the sink
a crumb-grained mirror
of the curtain's dumb in and out,

its lace-patterned border, even:
   Horse, church, dog, man.
   Horse, church, dog, man.

[PANDARUS:]

Slatternday Crumbday
Troilus gotten slow
as a story I have to read
aloud to the end of
like war's unhappy hover
fat water stain
(yep, still there)
on the ceiling

He calls from bed to tell me
the dog brought home
another owl carcass

Enormous eye pits! he says

Hey I tell him let's take a drive
to that bar on County X
sky cleaving in our wake
clouds wrecked in the treetops

May he says is a ruby in a casket

He'd rather park at Criseyde's
empty house her *disconsolate palace*

Troilus I want to tell him
that girl's mind is not
so grass-dazzling but I know
the feeling a griefly Should

like Yes there's no
good news coming

So for him I go
humming my red-bird song

[CRISEYDE:]

I didn't know who I was, we say,
didn't know what I wanted.

I knew: it was winter in me,
and the road taken from the cornfields

and the crow king of us. Then—
I was bemused, was loved.

It made me cruel, a little:
I dreamed of flower girls

painted in suet and birdseed
and the bows on their shoes

tied nothing in. There's a happiness
so hard you pray to be ripped from it,

to be dropped anywhere—
there, maybe: snow pulls to the ground

and you are sleeping.
Tires shush the street,

the wind tastes of pennies.
What I was, what I wanted.

The way a sparrow hawk
unthreading a lark on a marble floor is—

those pictures made me beautiful.

[TROILUS:]

I watched him paint all he could draw—

waves and fish and gulls—
on the walls of an abandoned beach house

with a stick tipped in ash,
the points of his spine shining

in his smooth back,
black hair fanning his olive neck.

I didn't know why I wanted
to be him and was not.

A commonplace: memory as *X*.
As: *wind at the door again.*

Another: *to make
of the mind a wolfishness, snarl*

of if / only / if.

For solace, I've been reading taxonomy.
In "The History of Animals," for example,

Aristotle says straight eyebrows
signal a soft disposition.

He doesn't mention joined.
That hers were suggests, Pandarus says,

a lack of discretion.

I told him: *it's rehearsal.*

Eight pills, each to its own thimble,
eight half-full tumblers of vodka

casting wavery halos down the kitchen table
like the sun-struck rungs of the ladder

off the pier. When I hit
the silt carpet, I mean to kick hard,

to clear the roof. By then I want everything
familiar as epitaph:

the wind and the water-lights and the little girl
who soldiers down the street

each morning at ten, arms swinging,
hands rigid. Today she's a brave messenger

in a green skirt and a bike helmet.
We were beautiful. Our heads were glass.

Three

And whan that he was slayn in this manere,
His lighte goost ful blisfully is went
Up to the holughnesse of the eighthe spere,
In convers letyng everich element;
And ther he saugh with ful avysement
The erratik sterres, herkenyng armonye
With sownes ful of hevenyssh melodie.

Chaucer, *Troilus and Criseyde* (V.1807–13)

[CHORUS:]

We tried to remember
what the letter said
the first time we read it

which is like trying to remember
the look of the city you live in
before you knew it too well.
Sometimes we sat for hours,

the clock loud on the kitchen wall,
the chair loose under our crossed legs,
and out there the watchfulness

of the trees, of the gray river.
There was some message,
a code we'd forgotten.
But what could we do?
What else can the mind do

with a map charting so much dark water?
At night, it turns the familiar colossal,
ungainly, tries driving its audience wild
with dreams. The heroes go down
singing. They go down

with mouths full of thorns.
There's the stage again,
and the smell of the house—
autumnal, heavy with smoke and leaf dust—

and there he is, calling out from the wings,
"Moon, you're so rich,
why don't you buy me something?"
And the moon sailing
into the curtain's blue folds.

[NARRATOR:]

Our usual consolation of daisies.
And yesterday, on Newhall, a Blue Angel
who tipped one wing across the length
of the paperboard factory before righting itself
just over the howl we were looking up through
the sunroof to, as though *yes, you down there,*
you are the ones. Our ears burned all the way
to Doris's solstice party, where "You can't tell
how late or light it is," Spoon said as he lit lanterns
in the garden shade, and Steve half-waved
the can of Miller resting on the shoulder
of the lawn chair next to him. How long
it seems, the three summers since his ex warned
if she ever did it, she'd swim across Lake Michigan
and the lake—though it took its own sweet
lacustrine time—obliged. It helps to imagine
what might love us beyond our skin
borrowing a minute's amber in the flush
off the neighbor's brick wall. To see,
one philosopher said, where there is nothing to see.
But what if we embarrass the dead, if they're sitting here
like guests whose names we can't pronounce,
all polite and cross-legged and "Wow, Nobody,
you really put your foot in it this time,"

I didn't add to the slant talk of begonias,
the joint making another round.
Or: *a ghost ship, many-masted, dogs us.*
Where, we keep answering the phone
in our deep sleep, *are you?* And the voice says
never is the dark long enough.

[CRISEYDE:]

Dear (you know I never
rode horses well)
late April, your sinkholes
in full bloom.
The bus bucks,
the windows shiver.

I've never seen a street
open a fabulous new crater.
I was walking elsewhere,
eyes small
against the wind.
Was, will be, whatever.

The last one, the one
that woke me?—
you could throw a ladder
down to hell.

Speaking of:
I've been reading
about Rodin's *Gates*.
How "the undulant topography
reifies the scrimmage
between *us* and *them*."
Which means, maybe,

that barred (in this life) entrance,
one turns back upon oneself
and finds that wow,
the hell we *can* know

is Really Quiet.
There's a dead mouse on its back
in a corner, toes furling,
and a bag of rotten ground beef
in the doorway
you have to step over.

A fly would be
a pretty measure.

Like finding,
in last month's snowbank,
an open tube of lipstick.

Same half-story out there—
soyfield, cornfield, wetland,
soyfield, Walmart.
Eagle on a road sign.
Hawk on a road sign.
Cowbird on, etc.

Yours, and sorry:
for a thin month,
my thin letter.

[TROILUS:]

What lean pickings
the body: like—
        oh, wood-char,
ochre, burnt coriander.

It was never like us.

If someone told you
it's nice here,
I want to be here always,
would you believe her?

Here: winter light in the kitchen
when the geese come so close
you think the sky
is passing through.

You think: things whisper
in a gladness beyond us.

I watched her play bride
in the mirror once,
pinning flowers
above the half-hearts of her ears.

Lift the veil, she said,
and her breath did, a little.

I tried to write her:

When you come
bring what canyons
you find
bring birds
cleared of wing
bring the bee
in its orchid catacomb

bring the whole
star-hive stilled—

In the story I dream
she sleeps through
all the nothing towns
on the bus south

and when she wakes
she takes my hand.

"What a year," she says.
"Worse than high school.

Two months. Then our friend X
was gone, too."

[CRISEYDE:]

I knew my would-be lover
for the plump sparrow
begging at the edge of my plate.
Invitation to the Province of Yes.

Brunch on the river-shadowed patio
of Café Europa—
mimosas in fishbowl glasses, violets
and a slick clutter of frisée in the salad.

The butter knife made my palm ache.
I'm sorry, I told him.
Maybe I'm too cold to eat.

On the terrace below us
everyone was ordering ice cream.

When I was a girl, fat and unworthy,
my mother taped a quote to the mirror
opposite my bedroom window.
"See yourself as others see you."
Hi, paper face, I told it.
Hello, halo of January oak,
its branches like crabbed marginalia
sprawling from my should-be head.
That's me at the table:
a black sundress,
its neck-stem bobbing.

Walk with me in the park, he said,
which means, of course, listen.
I did: the hiss of two kites tearing around
like Paolo and Francesca, he said.

Robins, chickadee, chick-a-dee-dee-dee.

I should've guessed.
A few towns over = the same birds
on the same page.
When he left, I sat on the bench,
still as Daphne.

Whom groundhogs came to parse.
Whose hair the green light roosted in.

[TROILUS:]

Nightfall when I crossed
the bridge over the river, and the river
gave off the smell of old stone,
which is the smell of our gods,
of their worn faces
in the museum's small light.

The sound they make! It's the sound
of perpetual sacrifice, of the mind
trying to be quiet. Even now something
is breathing in the disarray
of the peonies, and there—

in the plot where last month
the tulips stood like bright doors
to somewhere else. The yellow

and silver grass turns in the wind,
in the thickness and glitter of bees.
Yes, I'm still here, sweeping
up the pale hair caught
in the floorboards under
the shadow of the maple.

But I'm also remembering:
whole villages marched into the sea
and the green waves came
to greet us. In a clump of weeds
at the shoreline, a doll's head

marking our progress. No,
something smaller:
her eyes gone calling.

[CRISEYDE:]

By night my father's house shines
on the black river bank, all windows
and angled like a sail set on its side.

I tried to write him:
        In the park I walk through each dusk
a parliament of locusts
and the hot tongues of the paper mill upwind.

I tried:
        Dear thief of trumpets,
your complaints trail me
through these talkless rooms.

Just the sibilance and static
of the news behind the study door,

the shear of a plane
like the opening of some wild tantrum:
called from, not to.

When I arrived my father said,
of the broken capillary under my left eye,
How unsightly. It proves, honey—
(his only motto—though the hip's
healing anyway)—
it's for the worst everything changes.

It's not the story I want.
It's the first gold letter. It's margins
netted with willows and Blue Jays

and women reading to each other,
teacups perched on their knees—

Then she became a swallow.
Then she became a tree—

A commonplace:
The book gone on,
lovely without us.

[CASSANDRA:]

Now the accrual of was. At Booth Lake, the body
on the gold rocks in the shallows. And the horses
grazing slant on that hill. Every lake owns its own
tragedy. One ate water. One shut yellow eyes
to the sun. One said each star finds its best
socket. One said I didn't anyway have a daylight
face. One was: a pose and pause and lily pining.
One the radiant landing. One said the sentence
is the memory of the evoked world. One said
Orchard Street, Swamp Angel Road. One said
a window or scrap of graph paper drawn in cloud.
One was lithe-tongued, virtually. One said no one
asked you to sing. One sang here is a grass-blade
here is the sail distance calls faith. One said oh
but they never looked like real horses. One said
swallows the architects of. One said it isn't words
the mouth wants. One said Occasion. One said

Four

Allas, of me, unto the worldes ende,
Shal neyther been ywriten nor ysonge
No good word, for thise bokes wol me shende.
O, rolled shal I ben on many a tonge!
Thorughout the world my belle shal be ronge!
And wommen moost wol haten me of alle.
Allas, that swich a cas me sholde falle!

Chaucer, *Troilus and Criseyde* (V.1058–64)

[CHORUS:]

Then came the sand trucks,
the glass trucks, whistling
here, better put on a pair of these,
whistling: *ears palm-lodged,*

spoons idle, you were up to what
anyway, fingertips trolling for clues:
soft collapse of an ash pile, some
subatomic cackle.

We were running our thumbs
over the smooth girl in our compact,
like a contagion, the grain
of that skin, like: Are not

the plague cities also
beautiful? Churches sprang up
along canals, the porous everything
exhaled its dewy ghosts—

In the square, some light
that didn't know from history
or "the painterly dawn"
tacked about her—

fire-sailor, boat of so sonorous
a medium as belief.

We take the Hoan Bridge home
from the airport, the road salt mountain
to the west asleep under its tarp.
You miss the sun so long and then
my ex once said *it wastes the mirrors.*
Everywhere now a girl's hands

are blossoming on steering wheels.
Strong-thighed, my friends and I rode
those buoys like bronze sea horses.
SMOKE FIRE WIND WATER
promised the restoration company on the harbor.
In Kyoto we saw the Thunder God
and the Wind God fierce equally
on their cloud platforms. And I don't regret

the afternoon spent at the hotel's sidewalk café
pretending, over beer, we were people
we wouldn't like writing postcards:
Conquered subway! Sold the new novel!
You can travel with kids, sure,
someone said, but it's easier not to
have them. Only: houseless and unadorned,

listen, you have to name the exact point
at which—it's like high school always,
how is the next assignment—
you arrived at this sorry equation.

"Repentance," the famous author wrote,
"belongs to another world."

[CRISEYDE:]

If in any harbor
were a sail called Infidel, another
called Faith, say I came back,
say I found you

in a hotel you'd christened
"This Chameleon Glade":
green shag carpet, big views

of a frozen lake, cloud swells
the gulls can sound nothing of.
We drink too much,

play cards in bed,
the ice machine's thrum sentinel,
a soul dreaming us, kindly

it dreams us:
you drowse through gaunt noon—
snow's grate, the maid's cart

rattling at every step—
you who suffered yourself,
even in sleep, as wind will

an open book.

About judgment:
I was taught
God's vision is far,
is many-chambered,
like a fly's

or a gun's.
But love makes a city
over. It changes the picture.

Giddy April, lithe
and piss-puddled,
its wind proving
all the empty things.

Then summer,
tended to:
screens patched,
the front porch
painted a different blue.

In the long checkout
at Pick'n Save
I lean against him
while the wet streets
catch a coastal pallor,

the sky bird-deep
in what knitting-up-ness
it can. Some busy song—
like: *you remember,*
you were here.

[CRISEYDE:]

It was like the old world sent me a letter:
Darling, if you're reading this it means . . .

It did; I was.

My life in another licked river city:
grafittied band shell, water tower, cars.

On a block of cream brick buildings
the sky had moved into, a storefront

whose handwritten sign keeps promising
"Hometown diner! Open soon! New owners!"

The old ones haven't unset the tables.
Scuffed plastic cups on ketchup-smeared placemats,

empty coffeepot stuck to the counter.
Goodbye Book of Consolation.

Goodbye goldfinch who'd rather snuff itself
in the maple than *let me see you*

There are lies and there are promises,

Pandarus told me one afternoon at his shop.
He was letting the oil drain

from a half-dismantled motorcycle
hunched over the pan like a stricken jackal.

White wine on ice in a plastic cup
and the garage doors open,

my lawn chair trembling on the foot-wide lip
of broken concrete he called the patio.

Wasps owned the eaves over me, bees the field
of Queen Anne's lace and goldenrod

tall as my neck where I'd pee later. Afternoon, evening.
Troilus came, and when the waxing moon

cleared the neighbor's roof
Pandarus brought his father's old telescope out.

Except in books, I'd never seen the surface:
how precisely etched and sequined and sad-laked.

And the craters—their edges flaring
like the spokes of bone crowns, I said,

like the moon's a vault and the kings
will come back for them—

[CRISEYDE:]

The canister of Ajax glinting on the counter.
Just clear sky and elm light,

the floor an empty aquarium.
On Sunday we watched a man fish

a turtle from the lake.
He let it hang on his line, swimming

toward a rush of cloud. You can't
help it. Sometimes all the air

gets sucked from the air.
The turtle had a red undercarriage.

I looked and looked and couldn't
find my face in the mirror,

a girl passing our just-washed window
told her friend in the sundress.

Regnabo; regno; regnavi; sum sine regno.
Done with the lunch dishes, I think

my common thoughts: time to store
the winter coats, pay the dentist,

the doctor, Visa. On the tennis courts
across the street, the shirtless boys turn

and turn their shieldlike torsos to the sun.

[CRISEYDE:]

Daily it storms: dams give out, a lake in the next county
empties, every river swells. And the story says *this is love,*
this is hope, Silly. It's sorry, but it means to keep
the afternoon as I left it: folding chairs at a folding table
and the light wasp-colored, an old postcard of
this was a factory town. And *him* (who won't be *you,*
not again, nor still) setting the kettle on the ancient stove.
On the table, a receipt he'd written on—something
about God handing the world back to Job.

And the scent of it—enduring—called absence.
What kills the farmer's wife, the newspaper tells us,
is "it's beautiful, then it rains, beautiful, then it rains."
Because this is *The New York Times* their big red barns
"could rival a movie-set backdrop," and now that the sun's out,
the field-shimmer is "rain's strange effect." The land's full
of sky-blown holes where the corn sprouts will mature
enough or won't. Our grass palace—*this litel spot
of erthe*—in all its green's no ground for should.

[CHORUS:]

The way fences open
in a high wind, nothing
is at our disposal—

i.e., "Like the shy
of a horse's neck"
was the thought

drifting between us
when the road's patina
of wet tar and wet gravel

split. On the other bank,
the grass blew silver,
complicit, bent—

an afternoonish trick—
like boys at a tideline
digging, with their small shovels,

trenches. *Let the general's
fingers drum,* they sang,
let him shape out of smoke

lassos. A scythe of sky
rose with the water
at our feet: a star-trough,

a lost scramble
over tin roofs. Because
we said *breath*, we said *whose*.

Signed, thus, ourselves—
like the weather—Love,
your elaborate shore.

The second epigraph for the collection is from Seth Lerer's *Chaucer and His Readers* (Princeton: Princeton University Press, 1993). Lerer refers here to a cento written by Humphrey Wellys, "a Staffordshire lawyer and Tudor confidant who, in the 1520's and 1530's, put together a manuscript containing over sixty poems and prose pieces derived from Middle English examples." Each line of Wellys's cento is adapted from Chaucer's *Troilus and Criseyde*. According to Lerer, Wellys took great care that his manuscript should remain anonymous: not only did it contain propapal material that would be considered treasonous, but "rather than reading Chaucer and his heirs for their instruction in the arts of decorum, he looks into their windows on the indecorous." In the end, for Wellys "Chaucerianism has become the voice and vehicle for fantasy. The privacy of making has become the making of privacy."

"[Pandarus:] We made a sand woman on Harrington Beach": The bugs aren't crooning "It's Only a Paper Moon," written by Harold Arlen, lyrics by E.Y. Harburg and Billy Rose.

"[Criseyde:] Already I miss Troy": In the third stanza, the lines in italics are misquoted from Big Stick's EP *Drag Racing*. In both gesture and spirit, these are for Jeremy and Lynn.

"[Narrator:] Our usual consolation of daisies": The philosopher cited is critic Guy Davenport, the quote from his *The Geography of the Imagination* (Boston: David R. Godine, 1997): "About 2500 years ago poetry detached itself from the rituals of music and dance to go into the business of making the invisible visible to the imagination. This seeing where there is nothing to see, guided by mere words, is still the most astounding achievement of the human mind."

"[Criseyde:] I knew my would-be lover": the line "Whom ground-hogs came to parse" is, I'm nearly certain, remembered / recast from a source I can't recall.

"[Cassandra:] Now the accrual of was. At Booth Lake, the body": The phrase "a pose and pause and lily pining" echoes the refrain "A pause, a rose, something on paper" from Lyn Hejinian's poem *My Life* (Los Angeles: Green Integer, 2002).

"[Narrator:] We take the Hoan Bridge home": The famous author mentioned is J. M. Coetzee, the quotation from his novel *Disgrace* (New York: Penguin, 2000).

"[Criseyde:] If in any harbor": The line "But love makes a city" owes a debt to "Some Exquisite Sea Thing," the introductory chapter of Tony Tanner's *Venice Desired* (Cambridge, MA: Harvard University Press, 1992).

"[Criseyde:] The canister of Ajax glinting on the counter": The translation of the Latin phrase (which was often inscribed on depictions of Fortune's Wheel during the Middle Ages) is "I shall reign; I reign; I have reigned; I am without a kingdom."

"[Criseyde:] Daily it storms: dams give out, a lake in the next county": The quotations are adapted from Susan Saulny's article "In Midwest Floods, a Threat to Crops" (*New York Times*, June 17, 2008). The flooding described in the article took place in Iowa. Similar flooding plagued southern Wisconsin that spring.